simple
life

GUIDE

TO MOVING

CLOSER

TO GOD

THOM S. RAINER & ART RAINER

B&H
PUBLISHING GROUP
NASHVILLE, TENNESSEE

Custom for LifeWay Chrisitan Stores
978-1-4336-6867-8

Published by B&H Publishing Group and
LifeWay Research, Nashville, Tennessee

Dewey Decimal Classification: 248.4
Subject Heading: QUALITY OF LIFE \
STRESS MANAGEMENT \ LIFE SKILLS

All Scripture quotations are taken from the Holman Christian Standard Bible®. Copyright © 1999, 2000, 2002, 2003 by Holman Bible Publishers. Used by permission. Holman Christian Standard Bible®, Holman CSB®, and HCSB® are federally registered trademarks of Holman Bible Publishers.

Persons depicted in this book were part of a survey of 1,077 people and other interviews by the authors. In some cases several responses were combined to create composite accounts based on the data of the study. No actual names of the respondents are used in this book in order to protect their identities and confidential life circumstances.

Simple Life

You're probably too busy to read this book.

Yet for some reason you now have it in your hand. Perhaps the title intrigued you. Perhaps you've read other books we've written. Or perhaps you know that your life is not exactly the way you would like it to be. You are over-committed, overstressed, and underfunded.

You are looking for a better life: the simple life. You are not alone.

We have had the incredible opportunity to listen to more than one thousand people across America. They come from every geographic area, represent a diversity of races and ethnic groups, cross the age spectrum, and are nearly equally divided by gender.

Their stories are different, but at the same time they have similar concerns. Life is stressful. Life is busy. They don't have enough time for the things that really matter. And, most of the time, they feel financially stressed.

Jesus said, "I have come that they may have life and have it in abundance" (John 10:10). Yeah, right. Some of you may feel like you're barely hanging on. You would settle for just a mediocre life if you could get matters in some semblance of order. The abundant life seems to be a fantasy.

The apostle Paul said, "Rejoice in the Lord always. I will say it again: Rejoice!" (Phil. 4:4). You may roll your eyes at that verse. We heard from hundreds of people for whom joy had no reality in their lives. One of the respondents, a single mom who was forty-two years old, made her point powerfully: "I wish I knew how to have joy in my life. I am just trying to survive each day."

You probably have noticed that we are using Scripture quotations early in this book. We need to state our biases up front. We are both evangelical Christians. We believe that Jesus is the only way (John 14:6). We believe the Bible is the Word of God.

But, in this massive national study of how people saw and assessed their own lives, we heard from both Christians and non-Christians. Slightly more than one of five respondents is not a Christian, and even more are not evangelical Christians. We wanted to see if the perspectives on life were significantly different for the groups. We think you will be surprised at some of the responses. We were.

Our thesis is simple. We were not created to have miserable and joyless lives. We were created to have abundant and joyful lives.

But for most of us, such a life is elusive at best and seemingly impossible at worst. The two of us have listened to thousands of hours of interviews. We have heard the cries and, sometimes, the desperation.

For those who struggle we present the simple life. But first, let us hear from someone for whom life is anything but simple.

The Not-So-Simple Life

Maryanne is thirty-seven years old. She is married to Jeff, whom she met in college. They have two children at home: Franklin is eleven and Beth is nine. They live in one of the many suburbs of the Dallas/Fort Worth metroplex.

"I don't guess I should complain," Maryanne began. "I am blessed with a great family, and we do have our basic needs met. But, I have to admit, life is not very happy these days."

"Why?" we asked.

"You know the old cliché, 'You need to stop and smell the roses,'" she said. We nodded in affirmation. "Well, I am so busy and so worried I don't even know where the roses are," she laughed hesitatingly. "I have a decent job, a middle management HR position for a large company. The pay is steady but not great." Maryanne paused for a moment. She was measuring her words carefully.

"Jeff," she began slowly, "has not had the steady income that I have. He is a salesman for a local auto dealership. He's a good salesman, but the commissions are unpredictable. And the economy has not been that good for sales lately. We've had some pretty tough arguments over our finances lately. And I admit that I've been the one who has started most of the arguments."

We listened as she continued a familiar story.

"I also carry a tremendous amount of guilt about my role as a mom and a wife. I have to commute an hour and a half each day. When

I get home, I am exhausted. I really don't give the kids the time they need. And Jeff complains that I have no time for him for . . . well, you know."

We understood.

Tears began to well in Maryanne's eyes. "I can't believe I'm telling you guys this. It just seems that life is such a mess. It's a blur. I wish I could snap my fingers and everything would slow down."

At this point we were hesitant to ask further questions at the risk that we were piling on. So we asked the question with a bit of reservation, "Are you a Christian?"

"Wow, you guys are really sending me on a guilt trip." Her comment was terse, but she didn't seem angry. "Yes, I am a Christian. In fact, when Jeff and I first married, we were active in church. And I know that I should be taking Franklin and Beth to church. I know how important it was for me to be in church when I was a child."

Maryanne paused for a moment. "I guess if I just face reality, I have to say that I don't have time for God. I don't go to church. I don't encourage my family to be in church. My prayer life hardly exists, and I can't remember the last time I read the Bible."

We changed the topic to avoid further discomfort. But when we turned to the topic of finances, Maryanne's demeanor was no better.

"I told you that was a sore subject in my marriage." There was tension in her voice. "I get paid twice a month, and almost one whole paycheck goes to pay our mortgage. Jeff convinces me that we can put other expenses on credit cards until he gets a commission check. Well, those checks are slow in coming, and they are never enough to cover the full balance. It keeps growing, and the interest charges keep mounting."

We obviously opened a can of worms. Maryanne continued to talk with the decibels increasing.

"Jeff has no concept of saving. We have nothing set aside for the kids' college education, nothing set aside for future purchases, and nothing set aside for unexpected expenses. Nothing. Absolutely nothing. And he is considered self-employed but puts nothing aside for retirement. I don't put the maximum in my 401(k) because we need every penny just to pay our normal expenses. If we continue down this path, we will be paupers when we retire. Or we may never get to retire."

The interview was exhausting both for Maryanne and for us. We tried to wrap things up. But she had one last comment, a comment that was barely audible.

"I just wish my life would slow down. I just wish that somehow I could make my life simpler."

Maryanne's wish is what this book is about: a simpler life.

The Simple Revolution

Americans are rediscovering simple. At least they are aware that they need to rediscover simple. People are hungry for simple because the world has become so complex. The technology revolution has really become an overwhelming information revolution. We have access to more information, more products, more research, and more ideas than at any point in history.

We can plan an entire trip to another country with the punch of a few buttons. We can research the most complex topic without leaving our laptop. But the information revolution and the material abundance of Americans have made life more complex.

Thom Rainer and Eric Geiger wrote *Simple Church* a few years ago. They were amazed at the response. The book became one of the biggest best sellers ever in its genre. Why? Church leaders wanted simple. Church members wanted simple.

The more we saw the phenomenon of simple grow, the more we realized that the desire for simple is widespread. This book is being written on a MacBook Air instead of a PC. Why? Because Apple has discovered simple. We do all our Internet searches on Google. Why? Because it is so simple. We fly Southwest Airlines frequently. Why? Because booking, pricing, and travel are all so simple. And all of the wives in the Rainer family (four of them) received gift subscriptions to a single magazine. Its name? *Real Simple*.

But there is an overarching theme beyond the types of laptops we use, beyond the Internet search engines, beyond our travel plans, and beyond our reading preferences. We are searching for simple in our lives.

In the midst of the harried world of complexity, in the midst of uncontrollably complex lives, people want to find simple for their lives. They long for it, seek it, pay for it, and even dream of it. The simple-life revolution has begun.

As Christians, we are amazed at Jesus' earthly life. Despite the demands of the entire world on His life and time, Jesus found time to spend with His closest friends, His disciples. He found time to greet and hug little children. He found time to give one-on-one attention to those in need. And He found time to listen patiently to those who desperately needed someone to hear their deepest longings.

We know that we cannot replicate all that Jesus did, but we can pattern our lives after His. His life was many things, but it was clearly simple. He kept His focus and managed His time on what really mattered. And so should we.

The Study

We are not going to bore you here with all the details of the research we did for this book. At this point, however, we want to give you the framework for our study.

Our survey had forty-one questions that dealt with a plethora of life issues. The total number of respondents was 1,077. With a survey of this size, the margin of error is plus or minus 2.8 percentage points at the 95 percent confidence level. OK, unless you are a statistical nerd, those numbers are meaningless. In simple terms it means that our survey is very accurate.

We focused our research on those who still had children living at home, but the overall research applies to almost any life situation. We learned that many, if not most, Americans are looking for the simple life.

The respondents were fairly equally divided by gender, 57 percent female and 43 percent male. The age, racial and ethnic backgrounds, family income, and geographic diversity were pretty much a snapshot of United States demographics.

While eight out of ten of those surveyed said they were Christians, there was a wide range of religious or church involvement and denominational affiliation. We asked certain qualifying questions to classify a person as an evangelical and a born-again Christian. Only 35 percent of the respondents were born-again Christians, and even fewer, 11 percent, were evangelical Christians. We will dig into the responses of each of these subgroups later in the book.

What did these people say needed to happen in their lives for greater fulfillment? Simple. They needed simple.

When we concluded our study of these 1,077 individuals, we learned that they needed simple in four areas:

Time: They wanted simple so they could have time for areas of their lives that really mattered.

Relationships: Without a doubt many of the respondents struggled with balance in relationships. The simple life for them meant having better and closer relationships with others.

Money: Financial strains were pervasive with many in this study. They longed for a simple life free of past-due bills, limited income, deficient savings, and increasing debt.

God: These people, above all, saw a big void in their relationship to God. They saw clearly that they were too busy for God. They needed a simpler life in order to get closer to God.

We realize that many readers may have a greater concern with one or two of the areas above rather than all four of them. Feel free to turn to the section where you see your greatest need. In this book you will see four words again and again: Clarity, Movement, Alignment, and Focus. You will see the words in this chapter and in the introduction of each section. We think these concepts are important, so let us be clear what we mean.

Clarity

Clarity means that you know where you are going.

Before you move closer to a simpler life, you need a blueprint of where you are going. Many of you may not know where to turn because you have not made a plan to go anywhere. You need clarity.

We will challenge you in the first part of each section to develop a clear plan toward the simple life. We will call that the "Clarity Chapter."

- How do you plan on spending time on things that really matter?
- What is your plan for developing healthier relationships?
- How do you plan to get your finances in order?
- What is your plan for getting closer to God?

Clarity means that you have a plan and that the plan clearly states where you want to go. We will encourage you to write your own mission statement for each of the four areas: time, relationships, money, God. But don't leave those mission statements as inactive files on your computer. Make them the blue-print for the simple life.

We all know that we need clarity in these four areas, but most of the time we will not make a plan. Listen to the heartfelt cries of those we surveyed. You can hear their need for clarity.

- "I want to be able to spend more time with my child instead of working all the time and having him go to day care."
- "I would just love for kids to get along and quit fighting so we could have some peace in the house."
- "We really need a bigger apartment because we're very cramped here."
- "I wish we could manage our time better so we could spend weekends together."
- "I spend too much time taking everyone where they need to be when they need to be there."

- "I want a job that would satisfy all of our financial needs without taking time away from our family time."
- "We are constantly on the go due to our children's sporting events. Whether it's for practice, scrimmages, or games of multiple sports, we literally are gone from home almost every night of the week."
- "I wish we could pay off all our debt. It would take a lot of the stress off at home and allow us to spend more time together."
- "We all really need to be on the same page spiritually. Our relationship with God is an afterthought in our family."

We begin each of the sections with clarity. Simply stated, we help you see the path you need to travel. Many of those surveyed did not know where to begin. They need clarity, but there must be movement as well.

Movement

Congestion is rarely good. The word can take on different meanings, but few, if any, of them are good. *Congestion* means to be blocked up or to be too full of something. Congestion in the sinuses means you could have a headache or trouble breathing through your nostrils or you have a fever. None of those are good.

Congestion in traffic means that you aren't moving. Unless you planned well ahead, you are likely to be late. You get frustrated because too many automobiles are crammed into too few lanes on the highway.

Congestion is bad.

Congestion in life means you aren't making progress. You can have a clear plan of where you want to go, clarity, but you aren't moving toward the goal.

I (Thom) was forty pounds overweight for four years. The pounds crept on at the pace of about half a pound a month. It took almost seven years for the total weight gain of forty pounds to move me toward obesity, but it happened. Then I decided one day that I was going to lose the weight. I had clarity: lose forty pounds for greater health, stamina, and confidence.

But I stayed forty pounds overweight for four years. Why? Because I had no movement toward my goal. Wishing and hoping didn't get the job done.

Then one day I visited my youngest son, Jess, and his wife. He looked so slim and healthy, the best he had looked in years. I was both amazed and convicted. What had he done?

His response was simple. "Dad, Rachel (his wife) is cooking for me so I will eat healthier, and I am exercising regularly."

Hmmm. Eating healthy and exercise. What a novel idea!

Jess inspired me. I made commitments to eat better and exercise more. I removed the congestion. I had movement toward my goal. Today I am forty pounds lighter and feeling great.

In each of the "big four" areas of Time, Relationships, Money, and God, we will look at movement, how we remove the congestion to get where we need to go. But, for now, let us see some common elements in movement.

The first element is *intentionality*. We are sometimes asked how we write a book. We hate to admit it, but it is really simple. We decide that we are going to write a book, and then we begin researching and writing.

"No, wait a minute! We want to know the secret to book writing. Between the two of you, you have authored more than twenty books. Tell us the secret!"

Sorry, there is no rocket science here. We are just intentional. We act on our plan. Like Nike, we just do it.

After you have decided that you will make better use of your time, you act on your decision. You are intentional.

After you have decided that you have a purpose of better relationships, you act upon it. You are intentional.

You get the picture, don't you? The same is true for finances. And the same is true for getting closer to God. You are intentional.

Another key word is *incremental*. You don't try to conquer the world in a day. To add metaphor upon metaphor, how do you eat an elephant? One bite at a time. You create short-term steps. You have the clarity of where you want to go, but you don't try to arrive at your destination all at once.

We love the concept of Real Age. It started out as a book by a physician named Michael F. Roizen. Now it is a movement. The concept is simple (that word again!). Your biological age can be increased or decreased by many different factors. Those factors change your biological age to a real age.

For example, a thirty-five-year-old overweight man who smokes, never exercises, eats poorly, and has a family history of heart problems may have a real age of fifty-two. But a fifty-five-year-old man who takes care of himself physically and has no history of medical problems could have a real age of forty-eight. So the fifty-five-year-old man is physically younger than the thirty-five-year-old man.

Here is what we like about Real Age. You can go to the Web site www.RealAge.com and answer an hour's worth of questions, and it will give you your real age. Then it lets you know different steps you can take to become "younger."

Dr. Roizen is clear that you couldn't and shouldn't try to do everything at once. He advocates that you progress in steps. You may start with a mild exercise program. You may take a multivitamin. Or you may start eating healthier foods. You have literally dozens of choices, but you only take one or a few steps at a time.

You see, the Real Age experts know that if you try to do everything at once, you will become frustrated and give up.

That's the way it is with the simple life. Movement means you are intentional and you take incremental steps. You won't give up. You eat that elephant one bite at a time.

Now we have the clarity, our clear purpose toward simple. And then we have movement, how we will move from the complex life to the simple life. The next goal is alignment.

Alignment

You know the feeling. You are driving seventy miles per hour down the interstate. The road is flat and the surface is smooth. There are few curves; most of the interstate looks at you straight ahead. You can relax your hands from the steering wheel and the vehicle should handle fine.

So you let go for just a second. The car begins to veer to the right. You grab the steering wheel again.

In a few days your car is so badly out of alignment that you find yourself fighting to hold the vehicle steady. You can't put it off any longer. The wheels need alignment.

Since you are reading this book, there is a likelihood that your life is not in alignment. You are fighting the road. Something's wrong.

As we delve into the tough issues of moving toward the simple life, we look at areas where we go wrong, where our lives are out of line. And, most of the time, it only takes one small misstep to evolve into a major problem. Do you remember Thom's story of his forty-pound weight gain? He only gained half a pound a month. But in seven years he was obese.

According to the math of calories, he only overate the equivalent of one small piece of bread a day. But that small amount became a large amount over seven years.

Most people don't develop debt problems overnight.

Most Christians don't stop attending church suddenly.

Most relationships don't fail over one incident.

Most people don't become workaholics in one day.

Instead, their lives get out of alignment. It usually begins small. But it doesn't remain small.

We will share with you why the best of intentions get thwarted. In fact, we will let you listen collectively to more than one thousand people who shared their stories with us.

So you state clearly where you want to go (clarity). You begin to make incremental steps in the right direction (movement). You look at bad habits and problems that are interfering with your progress (alignment). Then you eliminate some good stuff.

Huh?

Yep, you read right. You eliminate some good stuff.

You see, it is one thing to get those bad habits and problems out of the way. But it is another thing to stop doing some good things. We call this last phase *focus*.

Focus

The year was 1985. I (Thom) was a student in seminary. My three sons were pre-school age. Art, the coauthor of this book, was three years old.

My studies at seminary consumed about forty hours each week, including fifteen hours in the classroom. I also served as the pastor of a small church and gave that church at least twenty hours a week.

Oh, the church paid me $50 a week. My wife, who was a stay-at-home mom, suggested that I find additional income. I listened to my wife.

I took a job at a bank where I had to work a minimum of thirty hours a week. And I almost lost my family and my sanity.

Can you name the bad things I was doing? Studying for the ministry? Serving as pastor of a rural church? Working at a bank to provide for my family?

But I almost lost my family and my sanity.

Many of the problems we heard in this study were not always the result of people doing bad things. Instead they were doing too many things, none of which by themselves were bad.

We looked at the lives of those who graciously participated in the study, and we saw many good intentions. We saw too many good intentions. We saw families take on activity after activity. We saw work lives that became workaholism. We saw the good become the bad because there was just too much of the good.

The simple life demands that we focus.

The apostle Paul said in Philippians 3:13–14, "But one thing I do: forgetting what is behind and reaching forward to what is ahead, I pursue as my goal the prize promised by God's heavenly call in Christ Jesus." One thing was Paul's focus: The goal of Christlikeness compelled him to move forward in his spiritual journey. In fact, for Paul, everything else was filth compared to this one thing (Phil. 3:8).

The simple life means that we eliminate some things in our life. It means that we have to make some tough decisions. In fact, focus may well be the toughest step toward the simple life. But it is absolutely necessary.

The intuitive sense of the MacBook Air is incredible. We are truly fans of Apple and the company it has become. Apple excels in simplicity because they are focused. Steve Jobs, the leader of the company, said he is "as proud of the things they have not done as he is of the things they have done."

Did you catch that?

He is excited because Apple said no. The company has made some tough choices, and they are better for it. They have focus.

Clarity. Movement. Alignment. Focus.

With these four you head toward the simple life.

Our Prayer for the Simple Life

This book was a tough project. Not because the research was daunting. Not because the writing was laborious, but because we heard so much pain. Because we heard about so many lives out of control. Because we heard cries of despair and voices of hopelessness.

Still we believe there is hope. We believe that the messed-up and complex life can become the simple life. We do not despair. And we want you to join us as we win and celebrate victories toward the simple life.

To that end we have prayed for you, the reader. We don't know you by name, but we know that the God to whom we pray knows everything about you. And by His power you can see despair become hope and confusion become simple.

Join us for the journey.

Join us for the victory.

Welcome to the simple life.

Moving Closer to God

Clarity → MOVEMENT →
Alignment → Focus

No one likes congestion.
We have never heard anyone say that one of his or her favorite moments is to be tied up in traffic for two hours.

And if you live in the Southeast like we do (Thom in Tennessee and Art in Florida), you are likely to experience a flight delay in the Atlanta-Hartsfield-Jackson International Airport. Wow, even the name of the airport is congested! In fact, we often plan flights so that we don't have to fly through Atlanta. The chances are great that we will be delayed getting in or getting out.

The reason? Congestion.

Oh, they will tell you that it is due to weather or some other reason, but the reality is that there is no margin for error or bad weather or anything else. The slightest glitch means that some of the planes will have to wait before they can leave to go to Atlanta (that wonderful airline-speak phrase called "ground delay"), or they will have to wait in a long line to depart.

Congestion is bad.

Both of us have allergies, but Art really has it bad at times. In fact, he has asthma. His airways constrict, becoming inflamed and lined with excessive amounts of mucus.

Excessive amounts of mucus? Ugh.

OK, we have made our point.

But the reality is the same. Congestion is bad.

The problem with congestion is that it hinders the best or most natural process or progress. We need to move in one direction but congestion stops us or detours us. We aren't our best or we can't do our best when congestion gets in the way.

Now let us ask you a simple question. Do you have congestion in your relationship with God? Perhaps you answer that question with a resounding no. That's great! But it's not the norm. In fact, our research shows that a significant majority of people readily admits that they need and desire a healthier relationship with God.

Let's look at some of the evidence. Nine out of ten of those surveyed believe in the importance of a spiritual foundation for them and their families. That's a lot. When you consider that 16 percent of the respondents indicated that they had no faith preference at all, the significance of the response is amplified.

OK, now we know that most people want a strong spiritual foundation. They want to get closer to God and to spend more time with Him. But how do they think they are doing? Not so great.

Nearly seven out of ten (69%) in our study desire more time for church and other spiritual matters. God is not in the picture in many lives. Congestion is in the way.

Jeannie is an artist who lives in Thom's hometown of Franklin, Tennessee, a suburb of Nashville. We asked her what she thought she needed to have a more complete life. Her response was straightforward.

"That's easy," she said quickly. "I would like to get closer to God."

So, we asked, where do you attend church?

"I don't."

How often do you read the Bible?

"Not much."

Do you pray regularly?

"Nope, sporadically."

"Look," Jeannie told us. "You can ask me questions all day about my spirituality, and I'm not going to fare well. That's what I'm getting at. I'm not close to God, but I want to be. And I really don't have a good excuse. I just have never made a habit of those things I know I should be doing. I'm too busy for my own good. I guess I'm too busy for God."

We earlier cited the apostle Paul's sole determination to get closer to God. But we need to be clear. Even Paul knew he had a ways to go. "Not that I have already reached the goal, or am already fully mature, but I make every effort to take hold of it because I also have been taken hold of by Christ Jesus" (Phil. 3:12).

Paul had not reached his goal. Paul was not fully mature spiritually. Paul had not arrived. But he didn't quit. In fact, he was able to move forward (there's that "movement" word) because Christ has already done the work. Paul could make every effort because his strength was Christ.

He could then say with confidence, "Brothers, I do not consider myself to have taken hold of it. But one thing I do: forgetting what is behind and reaching forward to what is ahead, I pursue as my goal the prize promised by God's heavenly call in Christ Jesus" (Phil. 3:13–14).

Paul had movement to get closer to God. He reached toward what was ahead. He pursued the goal. He removed the congestion and had clear movement toward God.

Notice what he said. He forgot what was behind. No, Paul did not have a sudden attack of amnesia. But he did say that he would no longer dwell on his failures. He knew that Christ had forgiven him, so he was ready to move on.

Ready to move closer to God in the simple life?

That's what we heard from the overwhelming majority. And now that you have clarity, a clear goal in mind, let's see what is next toward a closer relationship with God. Movement toward God can be summed in five words: *prayerful*, *forgetful*, *incremental*, *immediate*, and *resilient*. Let's look at each of these words.

Movement toward God: Prayerful

I (Thom) can't even pray without first being prayerful.

Yeah, I know, that sentence is totally confusing.

I struggle with consistency in my prayer life. I read about great prayer warriors who spent hours in prayer, and I am ashamed. I have trouble focusing for thirty minutes. I begin my conversation with God, and I often start thinking about my to-do list for the day. When I lose focus in my conversations with my wife, she lets me know quickly.

So I asked God to help me with my prayer life.

I prayed for a better prayer life.

In that same book of Philippians, Paul said, "Don't worry about anything, but in everything, through prayer and petition with thanksgiving, let your requests be made known to God" (Phil. 4:6).

You can't miss it. He said in *everything* let your requests be made known to God. Everything. Every big thing. Every little thing. Everything.

So now, my first step in a better prayer life is to pray for a better prayer life.

Simple? Yes. But profound.

God wants to take all our needs, our burdens, our worries, our cares. We are to take everything to Him in prayer.

In the previous chapter you established clarity. You set some goals that you would like to reach to get closer to God. We heard from Jack in the previous chapter. Jack's statement in that chapter made a perfect mission statement:

> *I will move closer to God by beginning to read the Bible at least fifteen minutes a day, by taking my family to church each week, and by talking about spiritual*

> *matters with my family at least once a week.*

It's a great mission statement. It encapsulates everything we said about clarity.

But the next step is action. Clarity must shift to movement. The goals must also be an action plan.

That's where we fail often, isn't it?

We plan to spend more time with the kids, but we don't do it.

We plan to lose weight, but we don't do it.

We plan to read the Bible, but we don't do it.

And we plan to get closer to God, but we don't do it.

Clarity says have a good plan. *Movement* says act on the plan. And that's often where the breakdown occurs.

That is why we begin with prayer. That is why we begin with God and not ourselves.

We are asking for His strength and not our own.

You have a great plan, but you are afraid of failure. Stop everything. Stop everything right now. Pause for a moment. Pray. Ask God for His success as you seek to get closer to Him. Stop depending on your limited ability and start depending on the One who has no limits.

Pray. Nothing moves congestion like prayer.

Movement toward God: Forgetful

I (Thom) absolutely love my wife, Nellie Jo. She is beautiful. She is godly. She is smart. She is fun. She is also blunt.

Nellie Jo does not mince words. Now hear me well. She certainly follows the biblical pattern of submission. She has followed me all over the nation. She has taken care of three boys while I pursued my goals and dreams. She always put the boys and me before herself. But that does not mean she lets me get away with anything.

For example, one of my greatest joys is spending time and talking with my three sons. They are now grown and married, but we still stay in touch almost every day. And when Nellie Jo hears me tell one of the boys that I will do something for him, she typically tells me that I will forget.

THOM: OK, Sam, I will send you that book.

NELLIE JO: No you won't; you'll forget.

THOM: Art, I will call him for you.

NELLIE JO: No you won't; you will forget.

THOM: Jess, I will send you a check for the tickets.

NELLIE JO: No you won't; you'll forget.

Sigh. I do forget a lot.

Then Nellie Jo tells me to leave Stacy (my assistant) an e-mail or voice mail so that she will remind me. Hmmm, does that mean Nellie Jo thinks Stacy is more diligent than I am?

Still, I can't argue the point. I do tend to forget too many things. I do get distracted.

You get the point, I'm sure. Forgetting is always bad. Right? Wrong.

Do you remember the words of the apostle Paul noted earlier? "But one thing I do, forgetting what is behind . . ." (Phil. 3:13). It's really amazing. The apostle talks about his singular focus in life, and the first thing he mentions is that he forgets.

You see, forgetting is not always bad. In fact, it can be positively life changing.

We often set goals. We often plan to get closer to God. We often think that this time it will work. But it doesn't.

We are paralyzed from moving forward because of past failures. Listen to Stephanie's story.

"I am a divorcee," she began with her eyes looking downward. "My husband left me three years ago. And he had every right to leave. I had an affair with his best friend. Well, I guess you would say his former best friend.

I can't explain myself to this day. I didn't love his friend. I loved my husband. I still love him."

Stephanie responded in our survey that she wanted to move closer to God. She had begun attending church, reading her Bible regularly, and praying every day. But then she stopped.

Why?

"I just feel like such a failure," she admitted. "I don't know if I can ever love or be loved again by anyone, including God."

Jesus encountered a woman who probably felt a lot like Stephanie. The story is in John 8:1–12. The woman in the story was actually caught in the act of committing adultery. The accusers brought her to Jesus. Their primary intention was to trap Jesus even more than shaming and accusing the woman.

The scribes and the Pharisees wanted to see if Jesus would really follow the law of Moses, which called for the stoning to death of one caught in adultery. So they asked Him what they should do with the adulterous woman.

Jesus was writing something on the ground, but for a moment He stood up and answered them, "The one without sin among you should be the first to throw a stone at her" (John 8:7). One by one, all the accusers quietly walked away. Only Jesus and the woman remained.

Jesus stood up again from His writing, and He spoke directly to the woman, "Woman, where are they? Has no one condemned you?" (v. 10).

Don't you wish you could have been there? Don't you wish you could have seen the expressions of those who left and the woman who remained?

She answered simply, "No one, Lord" (v. 11).

And Jesus, the One who is God, responded, "Neither do I condemn you. Go, and from now on do not sin any more" (v. 11).

Forget. Leave that behind. Go and sin no more.

Some of the respondents in our study just had trouble forgetting. They had trouble believing they could move forward.

Congestion precludes movement. Is it possible that some of the congestion you are experiencing is because you can't forget?

"He has rescued us from the domain of darkness and transferred us into the kingdom of the Son He loves, in whom we have redemption, the forgiveness of sins" (Col. 1:13–14).

He has forgiven. Now you must forget and move forward.

Movement toward God: Incremental

We keep returning to the mission statement of Jack for several reasons. For one, it is simple. For another, it is realistic. Jack does not state that he will read the Bible in its entirety every month, spend fifteen hours a week in prayer, and share his faith with at least twenty people each week.

Those goals are admirable. And in God's power, all things are possible. But most of us will become discouraged and frustrated if we set such lofty goals.

Jack's plans were to spend only fifteen minutes a day reading the Bible, take his family to church just once a week, and talk with his family about spiritual matters only once a week.

We can anticipate some of you superspiritual types dismissing Jack's plans as superficial or inadequate. But remember, this plan is a beginning, not an end. We will talk later about incremental movement, or eating the elephant one bite at a time.

For now you have clarity through your mission statement. You are beginning to act upon the mission statement. You began the movement with prayer. You then learned that you needed to forget the past and move toward the future. And now you are learning to move at a pace that is sustainable.

The simple life means that you enter into this process simply. If you have concluded that one of your main deficiencies in life is a closer relationship with God, start moving in that direction.

Have you ever seen a Christian meteor? She begins to get serious, real serious about getting closer to God. She spends fifteen hours a week at the church. She prays two hours a day. She reads the Bible two hours a day. She goes on three international mission trips in one year. And then she flames out. Totally burned out.

We are not discouraging you from a life totally committed to God. We are simply asking you to consider a slower, more incremental pace.

I (Thom) shared a few details of my weight loss earlier. I have been on many diets: low carbohydrates, extremely low calories, one-food diets, etc. They all failed for one simple reason: I tried to lose my weight as quickly as possible by dramatically changing my eating habits.

But this last time the weight came off and stayed off. How? I modestly reduced calories and modestly increased physical activity.

Today I'm walking as much as ten miles a day, but I didn't start that way. One mile a day was the beginning.

Now we don't mean to compare a diet with a relationship with God. But relationships often take time to develop, at least from our human perspective. Begin with a mission statement that is both simple and incremental. You will remove a lot of congestion that way. And one year from now, you may be surprised at the progress you've made.

Movement toward God: Immediate

Let's return to the story of the adulterous woman. Jesus clearly communicated to her that she was forgiven. But what then does

He tell her? "Go, and from now on do not sin any more" (John 8:11).

Notice what Jesus did not say. He did not say, "Give this serious thought and after a few weeks change your lifestyle." No, He told her to sin no more. Right then. At that moment. Without delay.

We have lots of statistics in this research. Reams of data. Page after page of numerical responses. So much that if we put just 10 percent of all the results here, you would have a book of statistics and graphs. And most of you would be bored silly.

So we spent hundreds of hours going through the data so you wouldn't have to do so. One of our main quests was to discern patterns. And we did discover several patterns, one of which probably won't surprise you. One of the main sources of congestion was "soon."

"I will start back going to church soon."

"I plan to begin reading my Bible every day soon."

"I will start talking about spiritual matters with my family soon."

Of course, "soon" never happens. It's put on the shelf of good intentions. But "soon" becomes "never."

One good example is that last quote: "I will start talking about spiritual matters with my family soon." For whatever reasons, people have a strong desire to talk about those issues that really matter but a desire that often does not translate into reality.

What is curious is that discussing spiritual issues is a big priority for most, yet only 23 percent of those who responded to our survey agreed strongly that they discuss such issues regularly in their families. It's the "want to" and "am doing" disconnect.

Meet Shelly from Wyoming. She considers herself a Christian. She and her family attend church "usually three times a month." Her plight is common.

"My family and I love to talk," she said. "We talk about school, work, football, the girls' boyfriends . . . almost everything but God."

The obvious question came next. Why?

"I really don't have a good answer. I don't believe there is anything more important to talk about. But we just never do. It seems awkward for some reason. Still, I keep telling myself that we will make spiritual matters a part of our regular talks, but I just never get around to it. I have good intentions, but I don't follow through."

The story is common. And it seems in two of the four big issues, God and money, it is more common. Movement is hindered by congestion, and one of the most common forms of congestion is procrastination.

The writer of Hebrews addressed this issue in an unusual way: "Watch out, brothers, so that there won't be in any of you an evil, unbelieving heart that departs from the living God. But encourage each other daily, while it is still called today, so that none of you is hardened by sin's deception" (Heb. 3:12–13).

Notice how the writer dealt with the idea of encouraging each other daily. He said do it "while it is still called today." Daily doesn't mean soon. Daily doesn't mean tomorrow. Daily doesn't mean when you get around to it. Daily means today, now, at this very moment.

You have established a mission statement. You thus have clarity. But a mission statement by its very nature requires action or movement. You have thus prayed for God to give you His strength to accomplish it. You have moved beyond past failures and sins. You have determined that you will take baby steps and not try to accomplish so much that failure is a near certainty.

Now you must simply do it. No excuses. No waiting. Just do it.

Movement toward God: Resilient

The apostle Paul provides an example for so many aspects of the simple life. In 2 Corinthians 11:24–28, he gives us a glimpse of the trials he endured:

> *Five times I received from the Jews 40 lashes minus one. Three times I was beaten with rods. Once I was stoned. Three times I was shipwrecked. I have spent a night and a day in the depths of the sea. On frequent journeys, I faced dangers from rivers, dangers from robbers, dangers from my own people, dangers from the Gentiles, dangers in the city, dangers in the open country, dangers on the sea, and dangers among false brothers; labor and hardship, many sleepless nights, hunger and thirst, often without food, cold, and lacking clothing. Not to mention other things, there is the daily pressure on me: my care for all the churches.*

Not such a pretty life, is it? But you know what Paul did. He always bounced back. He never gave up.

Why? He answers the question well. "So because of Christ, I am pleased in weaknesses, in insults, in catastrophes, in persecutions, and in pressures. For when I am weak, then I am strong" (2 Cor. 12:10).

Paul was truly resilient.

The simple life means that we start taking some serious steps toward getting closer to God. But, for some of you, the fear of failure is just too great. You've tried in the past. And you've failed. You tried. You failed. What's the use of trying yet again?

Margaret is from upstate New York. She speaks for many of our respondents. "I know some of the things I should be doing," she began. "But I also know that any efforts I make will end in failure. I said I would read the Bible every day. I failed. I said I was going to have a daily prayer time. I failed. I said I would attend church at least once a week.

I failed. Why should I expect that I'll get it right this time?"

Movement means that we try again. And if we fail, we try again. It means that we are resilient and do not give up.

Not too long ago, one of the most viewed YouTube videos was "The Last Lecture" by Randy Pausch, a professor at Carnegie Mellon University. Though we would like to have seen a greater emphasis on eternal life, the story of Randy Pausch is one of the most compelling visions of the simple life and never giving up.

Pausch, at age forty-six, was diagnosed with pancreatic cancer. Instead of going into a shell and giving up, he continued to live his life to the fullest. He could have had a pity party that he would be leaving a loving wife and three young children. He could have said that life isn't fair. He could have been angry. He could have given up.

"The Last Lecture" is just that. It is Randy Pausch's final lecture at the university where he served as professor. And what is amazing about the lecture is the indomitable spirit and the incredible attitude of this man. One of our favorite quotes from Pausch in this final lecture is: "I have fun every day of my life, and I am going to continue to have fun every day that I am alive."

Randy Pausch died on July 25, 2008, at age forty-seven. But he never gave up.

Movement and Getting Closer to God

Now let's review the pattern we have so far of the simple life. The first step is *clarity*. We even suggested that you write a mission statement about your intentions. And we gave you an example of one man's mission statement for getting closer to God.

The second action is the subject of this chapter, *movement*. Movement is the removal of obstacles or congestion.

The big stumbling block in the early phases of the simple life is movement. Why?

Movement means we have to change our habits. And by our nature, we are creatures of habit. How many of you drive the same path to work? Do you eat the same type of unhealthy foods each week? Do you spend more time watching television than you do reading the Bible? Do you work so many hours that the kids get shortchanged?

Work habits. Eating habits. Leisure habits.

Movement means that you have to break many of those habitual patterns. Why aren't we moving closer to God? We have not broken enough habits to have time for Him or His Word. Perhaps we have declared Sunday a sleep-in day rather than getting to bed earlier on Saturday night so that we can attend church. Perhaps we give more lip service to that which really matters. But talking does not get the job done. We have to break out of the patterns that hinder us.

Also movement means immediate. If you are reading this book and you begin to think, *That sounds like a good idea; I might try it in a week or so*, you have missed the point and failed to move to the simple life. We heard many of those surveyed say that they plan to "get around to it" soon. But those "roundtoits" are the cries of failure. Movement means right now, not tomorrow but now.

Is there really anything more important than getting closer to God? If you have read this far in this book, you probably have formulated in your mind or, for some of you, in writing, a mission statement for moving closer to God. So you really are a person of serious intentions.

Now is the time to begin. Break the habits that hold you back. And make the decision in God's strength to do it now.

APPLICATION
SIMPLE LIFE: MOVEMENT
THE PRIORITY OF PRAYER

Look at Philippians 4:6: "Don't worry about anything, but in everything, through prayer and petition with thanksgiving, let your requests be made known to God."

Before you go any further, take time to pray. Pray that God will draw you closer to Him. Pray that you will practice those spiritual disciplines that will draw you closer to God. Pray that God will use this book on the simple life as a resource for a life closer to Him. Pray that God will give you His strength to move closer to Him *right now*.

Take a few minutes to pray.

Now answer the following questions from Philippians 4:6.

1. How is worry related to prayer?

2. What does it mean to present "everything" to God in prayer?

3. How does thanksgiving relate to prayer?

About the Authors

Thom S. Rainer is the president and CEO of LifeWay Christian Resources, one of the largest Christian resource companies in the world. Also a respected pastor and researcher, he has written more than twenty books and is the best-selling coauthor of Simple Church. Rainer and his wife, Nellie Jo, have three grown sons and live in Nashville, Tennessee.

Art Rainer serves on the staff of First Baptist Church of West Palm Beach, Florida. He is an MBA graduate of the University of Kentucky, and is currently pursuing a doctorate in business administration. He is married to Sarah.

simplicity.